THE STEAM RAILWAY SERIES VOLUME 4

Over The Pennine Fells

THE SETTLE AND CARLISLE LINE

Colin Walker

OXFORD ILLUSTRATORS LIMITED

First Published 1972

Printing B.H. Blackwell Printing Department Oxford

902280 06 6

Publishers Oxford Illustrators Limited 108 Cowley Road Oxford

Over The Pennine Fells

So much has been written about the former Midland Railway's route across the Pennines that one almost feels that all there is to say has been said. In detached factual terms this is perhaps true but on a personal level the line offered such a deeply individual experience that anyone who knew it more than superficially was left with an impression that was both powerful and lasting.

It was impossible to photograph the 'Settle and Carlisle' without beginning with the landscape, for the landscape dominates all. There are few places between Helwith Bridge and Kirkby Stephen where one can concentrate attention solely on the railway without being distracted by the overwhelming scale of the terrain it passes through. It is a scale that reduces the line and the wonder of its construction almost to the point of insignificance.

To 'happen' upon it when travelling through the northern dales can come as quite a shock. Among those frowning table mountains like Pen-y-ghent, Ingleborough, Whernside and Wild Boar, whose grit-topped peaks so determinedly resist the sculpting of nature, a railway seems quite out of place and even an impertinence when it is a main line laid out for high speed running. That it is a main line in the fullest sense of the term makes it one of the wonders of our railway system.

The line commences at Settle Junction where it parts from the Lancaster route to continue northwards through Settle and up the valley of the Ribble whose natural excavation it is pleased to follow, climbing at a gradient of 1 in 100. Passing through the gorge at Stainforth the route becomes steadily more impressive as the high hills begin to close in. At Horton in Ribblesdale it warily passes the first of the great Pennine bastions, Pen-y-Ghent, while three miles further on at Selside it skirts the fringe of that group of fells that rise Westwards to culminate in the mountain of Ingleborough.

The assistance of the river valley has already been abandoned by the time the line reaches the head of Ribblesdale and after passing the quarry and station at Ribblehead it is thrown across the expanse of bog known as Batty Moss on a splendid twenty-four arch limestone viaduct, a quarter of a mile long. No longer now does the railway evade the high hills but instead heads towards them in a direct confrontation. Curving below the mass of Whernside it proceeds up the fold of Little Dale and then plunges into Blea Moor, under which it tunnels for nearly a mile and a half. The summit of the northern climb is reached inside the tunnel at a height of 1,151 feet above sea level,

The next 10 miles are magnificent as the line is carried high along the Eastern slopes of Dentdale, crossing two more exquisite viaducts and passing through Dent station; then, curving north-east, it burrows below the rounded moor of Rise Hill through another tunnel three quarters of a mile long, to reach Garsdale where, in steam days, advantage was taken of the level gradient to install water troughs—the highest in England. At the head of Garsdale the line curves back again over yet another viaduct to find its northern exit from the fells, reached after a series of short tunnels at the line's ultimate summit of 1,169 feet at Ais Gill. Here, at the head of the dale known as Mallerstang Common where the River Eden commences its journey northwards to Carlisle and the sea, the fell of Wild Boar stands as a formidable sentinel over both the dale and the line, which has already begun its long descent towards Kirkby Stephen and to the softer, lusher pastures of the lower Eden valley. Viaducts and tunnels punctuate the journey from time to time but none of them rival those masterpieces of the high fells.

Unlike the short, sharp northbound climb of nearby Shap where many steam trains used to receive banking assistance, the 1 in 100 ruling gradient of the Settle and Carlisle line was deemed, latterly, to be within the capacity of a single engine and loads were usually adjusted accordingly. The prolonged 15 mile struggles that trains had to make to climb into the fells from both directions, however, made it a gruelling test and an engine with a boiler that was reluctant to boil was soon in trouble. Small wonder the line was nicknamed 'The Long Drag'! Moreover, the fickle extremes of weather and the line's wild remoteness made its operating a continuous battle against natural forces. 'The Weather' was no topic of idle gossip up there. It was an obsession and the running of trains was conducted with a strategy that kept one eye on the cloud base and wind direction, but still the weather occasionally won.

Not a few times, when taking cowering refuge beneath one of the line's bridges from the torrential storms that are so characteristic of the area, I was led to wonder just who were those men who pitted their strength and skill against such an environment and what was their brand of courage? What kind of a giant must John Sharland, the lines surveyor, have been to have walked the route over the fells to plan this flimsy thread of communication? Also, who are we now to spurn the magnificent efforts of such men by summary acts of closure?

To really know the Long Drag one had to 'live' it. To clamber over the fells, scale their dry stone walls, be caught in their storms, lost in their mists, squelch through their bogs, endure their blizzards and perhaps even discover the unfortunate laxative effects of drinking from some of their streams! The enjoyment of acquaintanceship was often tempered with a respect that bordered upon fear. The affinity between the hills and the sky above them was ever present even on the finest of days and in the lulls between trains it was to the sound of water that one always returned as it streamed down from the fells to disappear over falls or into thirsty, gaping holes. The night hours could be charged with an eerie mysticism. One remembers camping alongside the ominously named Hell Gill near the line's summit at Ais Gill and being kept awake either by the sounds of the freight trains wearily climbing up Mallerstang Common in a darkness that was total or by those of the gill, 'boiling' out from its crevice, 60 feet deep, where earlier one had noticed the rotting carcases of uncautious moorland sheep wedged tight in its grip.

Disturbed, if not such macabre, nights were a common experience near the Long Drag even in the comfort of a bed and within the security of the district's hospitable lime or gritstone walls. The trains themselves invariably thwarted one's attempts to sleep. Particularly notorious was the Station Inn at Ribblehead which lay shielded from the West winds by the section of railway embankment separating the station at Ribblehead from the viaduct. As train after train climbed past in the darkness it was usually too much of a temptation not to forsake the warm sheets in order to watch the sparks being thrown high by the assortment of engines that fought their individual battles with the final stages of the climb from Settle. In windy conditions one could hear its effect as the train caught its full impact on the exposed viaduct and the beat of the engine would slow and perhaps sharpen—if it had the steam to spare! One felt a distinct sense of relief when the brake van tail light disappeared which meant that the train had gained the cutting where there was some protection for the last mile to the tunnel.

Nights spent at Castlethwaite in Mallerstang Common were little better, Though a mile from the line, the massive efforts of southbound trains bursting out from Birkett Tunnel would jerk one back from the frontiers of sleep as they assaulted the climb to Ais Gill and both the curvature of the line and its brief changes of gradient were clearly transmitted by the engine's exhaust. One such change was the easing of the 1 in 100 to 1 in 330 past the signal box at Mallerstang, situated way up on the hill-side well over a mile from the nearest road; with access to it only possible across the fields. Mallerstang only opened at night in recent years and must surely represent one of the most lonely night shifts for a signalman in the whole of England.

The concern that one felt at the progress of trains was also shown by those signalmen whose boxes were situated, like Mallerstang, on the climbs. They didn't simply check the trains that passed them but they carefully scrutinised the activities and countenances of the engine crews who in turn would usually communicate by nod or gesture something of the state of affairs on the engines they were working. It was very much a shared experience and it brought the swift realisation that this was no ordinary railway.

Nor were the men of the 'Long Drag' ordinary people. The challenge of working such a line bred some fine characters among station staff, signalmen and permanent-way men and their existence, far removed from large population centres, made for a strong community spirit which extended over the whole line. Most of them dwelt close to it in austere looking railway properties that were ruggedly built to withstand the extremes of weather. Their pleasures were simple by the standards of the city dwellers but their knowledge of Pennine lore was sometimes deeply profound and they were pleased to share it with those who were interested. One was not long in the company of George Horner, one of the Blea Moor signalmen, for instance, before being treated to a discourse on the art of fly fishing with illustrations from his current collection of flies which he manufactured with such remarkable delicacy during the slack periods when there were no trains on the 'up–along' or the 'down-along' to disturb his concentration.

If the hours of darkness were sometimes awe-inspiring the Pennine dawn and sunrise could be a sheer delight in Spring and Summer. To watch the shapes of the great hills emerge from the lightening sky and to hear them come to life as the curlews and peewits got up and gave voice along with the moorland sheep was a precious experience. A small procession of trains came up from the South soon after six—the first was usually the morning parcels from Bradford followed by two or three freight trains. There was also the early workman's train from Helifield to Garsdale which returned after the engine had run round its train and transferred to the up line. Then, occasionally, during the holiday season they might all be preceded by a late running car-sleeper train to Scotland. It was worth the effort to be up for them and nothing so effectively galvanised one into wakefulness than the distant sounds of these trains struggling up Ribblesdale over rails whose smooth, cold, surface collected a constant film of water as they condensed the heavy morning mist. The car-sleeper was a particularly tough assignment and more than once I have listened anxiously at Ribblehead to a 'Britannia' Pacific coming up past Selside being worked to the limit of its adhesion by a driver who was striving to contain its desire to slip as he coaxed it on with its heavy load of coaches and vans.

Again, it was the combination of remoteness, landscape and altitude that gave the area its exceptional acoustic qualities and in some weather conditions trains were audible for nearly twenty miles. I have sat in the early morning high above the line on Widdale Fell overlooking Dentdale and the viaduct spanning Arten Gill and listened to a train approaching for fully 15 minutes as it climbed the neighbouring dale to Blea Moor when its entry into the tunnel abruptly silenced it. Its approach then became visual as one after the other the tunnel air shafts plumed with smoke as a prelude to its appearance and passing, after which its sound continued to persist intermittently until it was well on its way down Mallerstang Common, which channelled and amplified its sound back upon the air.

1 A Stanier 8F No. 48084 visibly accepts the challenge of the long climb to Blea Moor as it leaves Settle with a down freight train.

The Settle and Carlisle was a wonderful railway to photograph and it was fortunate for the photographer that it was one of the last lines over which steam found regular employment. Certainly steam engines never displayed themselves to better advantage than in those fells and every engine that ever climbed to its summits from North or South confirmed not only its own triumph but also the triumph of those whose tenacity brought such a railway into being.

2 A Stainer Class 5 No. 45120 travels light engine through the Stainforth gorge on its way to Carlisle.

3 A characteristic climb by 'Jubilee' class No. 45562 'Alberta' passing Selside with the 10.17 a.m. from Leeds to Carlisle.

4 An 8F No. 48714 lays a heavy smoke over the tiny signal box at Selside as it toils past up the grade.

5 'She's not doing so well, George.' Signalman Bill Thistlethwaite at Selside reports to his colleague at Blea Moor box on the uncertain progress of a Northbound freight train.

6 Two platelayers clearing snow pause to watch Class 5 No. 45106 as it departs from Ribblehead with the morning local from Carlisle to Hellifield. Behind the train and lost in the mist is Whernside.

7 The early morning sun catches 'Britannia' Pacific No. 70017 'Arrow' as it climbs past Ribblehead with a car-sleeper train from Sutton Coldfield to Stirling.

8 A Class B1 4–6–0 No. 61319 from York in the North Eastern Region is pressed into service because of a derailment at Hellifield. It is seen making a magnificent effort near Ribblehead with an express freight train.

9 The early morning workmen's train from Hellifield to Garsdale curves away into the mist from Ribblehead and approaches Batty Moss viaduct. On the right is the Station Inn.

10 and **11** 9F climbs. Two down express freight trains approach Batty Moss viaduct.

Ribblehead Viaduct

12 The massive construction of Batty Moss viaduct showing the huge bl[illegible] of local Great Scar limestone.

13 The delicacy of the viaduct in its wider setting. An Ivatt Class 4 2– crosses with a ballast train.

14 In the fading light a late evening up parcels train headed by a Stanier Class 5 swings down the grade over the viaduct. In the distance the flat topped mountain of Ingleborough rises massively from the dale.

15 The cloud base 'froths' over the summit of Whernside as a 'Britannia' Pacific crosses the viaduct with a car-sleeper train soon after sunrise.

16 Blea Moor's down distant signal clears for a Class 5 which has just shut off steam after crossing the viaduct with a freight train for Carlisle.

17 Ingleborough and its companions are lost in the early morning mist thus adding to the loneliness of a 'Crab' 2–6–0 battling wearily away from the viaduct with another down freight train.

18 An 8F 2–8–0 No. 48684 hauls a heavy Northbound freight train round the curve towards Blea Moor on a Summer afternoon.

19 A 'Britannia' Pacific No. 70053 'Moray Firth' approaches Blea Moor with the down morning express from Leeds to Glasgow.

45588

20 'Jubilees' at work. No. 45588 'Kashmir' relegated to freight duty displays its contempt by rattling the down morning pick-up goods round the curve to Blea Moor at express passenger speed.

21 Properly employed. No. 45693 'Agamemnon' looks very determined as it drags the 7.50 a.m. express from Derby to Glasgow over the last lap to the tunnel.

22 Little freight traffic actually originated on the Settle and Carlisle line and the majority that did came from the various quarries at places like Horton, Ribblehead and Long Meg. Here the down train of empties for Long Meg hauled by 9F 2–10–0 No 92233 approaches Blea Moor and passes sister engine No. 92019 which is waiting in the loop with the up loaded train of anhydrite.

23 The firemen of a North Eastern Region A1 Pacific, No. 60134 'Foxhunter' obliges with a telephone-arranged smoke as his engine nonchalantly lifts a featherweight summer Saturday special towards Blea Moor.

24 Signalman George Horner at Blea Moor.

25 'Jubilee' No. 45569 'Tasmania' tolls past Blea Moor box with a North-bound relief express for Glasgow.

26 The down Bradford parcels passes Blea Moor box with a Class 5 in charge soon after a grey dawn.

27 Taking the plunge. The fireman of Rebuilt 'Patriot' Class 4–6–0 No. 45531 'Sir Frederick Harrison' snatches a glance at the camera before his engine dives into Blea Moor tunnel with the 9.50 a.m. from Manchester to Glasgow.

28 Another on the way up. One of the tunnel ventilation shafts high up on Blea Moor releases smoke after the passage of a train while far away in the distance the next train can be seen making its climb below the brooding mass of Ingleborough.

29 Looking North from the top of Blea Moor over Dentdale where a train can be seen running along the slope of Widdale Fell having just crossed Arten Gill viaduct. On the left is the dark shape of Rise Hill beyond which in the distance lies Baugh Fell and finally the summit tip of Wild Boar.

30 A Stainer Class 5 No. 44726 roars o
of the North end of Blea Moor
tunnel and into Dentdale.

31 After travelling along Dentdale a
rebuilt 'Patriot' class 4–6–0 No. 455
'Sir Herbert Walker K.C.B.' curves
enter Blea Moor Tunnel with the
8.35 a.m. express from Glasgow St.
Enoch to St. Pancras.

32 Two more trains in Dentdale. A 'Clan' Pacific No. 72006 'Clan Mackenzie' dashes over Denthead viaduct with the Summer Saturday 8.25 a.m. express from Heads of Ayr to Leeds.

33 Sunrise splendour. A Stanier Class 5 with the down Bradford parcels train is caught by the sun as it shafts down the cleft of Arten Gill.

34 Another Class 5 hurries over Arten Gill viaduct with a down express freight on a Summer evening

35 On a morning of bleak mist a Stanier 8F hastens through Dent station with a Northbound freight train.

36 In pouring rain another 8F No. 48472 roars through Garsdale station with an up mixed freight train.

37 In rather better weather a 'Jubilee' No. 45646 'Napier' passes Garsdale in the opposite direction with an express freight. Behind the train is Baugh Fell.

38 The morning local train from Carlisle to Hellifield coasts round the curve into Garsdale with a Class 5 in charge.

39 A 'Crab' 2–6–0 clanks briskly through Garsdale with a freight for Carlisle.

40 From the Hawes-Sedbergh road at Garsdale Head an 8F is seen crossing Dandry Mire viaduct with the Long Meg empties. In the making of the Settle and Carlisle line Dandry Mire was an unscheduled viaduct—the railway at this point having been planned to use an embankment. However, owing to the bog's voracious appetite when attempts were made to make a foundation for an embankment the plan was abandoned in favour of a viaduct.

41 Hurrying South across the viaduct is 4F No. 44197 with a rake of coal empties.

Ais Gill

42 Ais Gill signal box. The highest building on the Settle & Carlisle with appropriately the highest heap of coal —a reminder of high altitude Winter seige conditions.

43 Summit in sight. A 'Britannia' Pacific on an up freight climbs the last few yards to the summit and prepares to take things a bit easier.

44 'Jubilee' climbs. The fell of Wild Boar towers above No. 45697 'Achilles' as it climbs to Ais Gill summit in fine style with a Southbound fitted freight.

45 Trying hard to live up to its name No. 45731 'Perseverance' makes heavy going of the gradient with a late running and overloaded 'Thames-Clyde' express.

46 The Ais Gill itself is situated almost a mile from the summit to which it gives its name. Here, crossing the gill is 'Jubilee' No. 45613 'Kenya' working hard with a relief to the up 'Thames-Clyde' express.

47 A 9F 2–10–0 brings a stone train from the Long Meg quarries up to the summit.

Class 5 climbs

48 With some steam to spare a Class 5 makes a massive last effort to the summit with a heavy freight.

49 Another storming climb by No. 45495 passing beneath the road bridge with an up freight.

50 No. 45236, steaming well, on the last lap.

51 As dusk falls a Class 5 with a train of fitted vans for the South approaches Ais Gill's down distant signal near the summit.

52 The up 'Long Meg' again—this time making steady progress with 9F No. 92119 at the front end

53 The rain pours down the curves of boiler, tender and carriage roofs as 'Britannia' Pacific No. 70054 'Dornoch Firth' hauling the up 'Waverley' express is caught in a torrential storm on its way up to Ais Gill.

54 Trains also went down the grade. The fireman of a 'Jubilee' Class 4-6-0 scatters the tea leaves from his billy-can as his train speeds down the hill towards Birkett tunnel.

55 The fireman of 'Crab' 2–6–0 No. 4288 takes some rough relaxation while his engine rattles into speed near Mallerstang.

56 A Class 5 on an evening freight for Carlisle wastes no time on the descent and leaves a steam trail from its safety valves between Birkett tunnel and Kirkby Stephen. Low, threatening cloud is driving quickly in from the North west.

57 The last vestiges of daylight clinging to the top of Mallerstang Edge provide just enough illumination to pick out the silhouette of a Class 5 as it climbs steadily towards Birkett tunnel with a Southbound freight.

58 From down in Mallerstang dale a Class 5 is seen high up on the fell side heading for Ais Gill with an express freight from Carlisle.

59 Steam Gone. Near Kirkby Stephen.

Other titles in THE STEAM RAILWAY series:

Oxfordshire Remembered
Shrewsbury
Kings Cross

In Preparation:

Birmingham and the Black Country (1)
Southern to the South West
The Border Cities Carlisle and Newcastle
Calling at Leamington
Grantham
Rugby
Welsh Border Wanderings
York
Shap and Beattock
Lines into Cambria
The Great Central